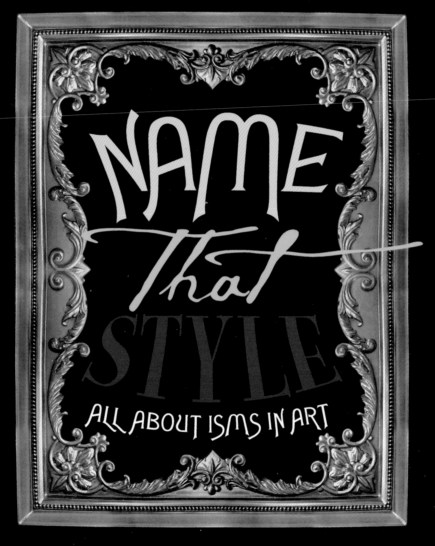

NAME That STYLE

ALL ABOUT ISMS IN ART

By Bob Raczka

M MILLBROOK PRESS / MINNEAPOLIS

To Pat, because I like your style

The country listed after each artist's name is the country in which the artist was born. Some of these artists traveled in the course of their careers, and a few did the majority of their work in a country other than their birth country.

Millbrook Press
A division of Lerner Publishing Group, Inc.
241 First Avenue North
Minneapolis, MN 55401 USA

For reading levels and more information,
look up this title at www.lernerbooks.com.

Library of Congress Cataloging-in-Publication Data

Raczka, Bob.
  Name that style : all about isms in art / by Bob Raczka.
     p.   cm.
   ISBN 978–0–8225–7586–3 (lib. bdg. : alk. paper)
      1. Art movements—Juvenile literature. I. Title.
   N5303.R29 2009
   709—dc22   2008000312

Manufactured in the United States of America
7 - 45602 - 8505 - 5/6/2019

INTRODUCTION

Looking at art is easy. But sometimes understanding art can be hard, especially if you don't know the words used to describe it.

For example, most people have seen Edvard Munch's famous painting *The Scream.* But if I said this painting was a great example of Expressionism, would you know what I meant?

Let me start by explaining what an ism is. In the world of art, a word ending in *ism* is a word that describes a style. Naturalism is one style. Cubism is another.

An ism can also describe an artistic movement. A movement happens when one artist's style catches on with other artists. Pablo Picasso and Georges Braque invented Cubism, but it became a movement, spreading to artists all over the world.

In this book, I hope to explain, as simply as possible, the ideas behind fourteen different artistic styles. Thirteen are isms, and one is not. But all of them are fascinating ways in which artists have looked at the world.

Jan van Eyck · *The Arnolfini Portrait* · 1434 · The National Gallery, London, England

What is Naturalism?

Naturalism is the easiest style to understand. It means the artist paints things realistically, without distorting them. Naturalism is not limited to a specific time period. It has been around throughout the history of art.

When and where was Naturalism popular?
Naturalism was very popular during the Renaissance. This rebirth of art and learning began in Italy and spread across Europe between 1300 and 1600. The invention of linear perspective helped to make Naturalism possible. So did the development of oil paints, which allowed artists to capture the colors and textures of real life.

Who are some of the most famous Naturalist painters?
Giovanni Bellini, Italy, ca. 1430–1516
Pieter Bruegel the Elder, Flanders, ca. 1528–1569
Jan van Eyck, Belgium, ca. 1390–1441
Leonardo da Vinci, Italy, 1452–1519

What are some of Naturalism's most important characteristics?
–portrays the world realistically
–shows human feelings and emotions
–natural settings
–uses linear perspective
–represents light and texture convincingly

Why is this painting a good example of Naturalism?
Jan van Eyck was one of the first artists to perfect the use of oil paints in a Naturalistic style. *The Arnolfini Portrait*, his painting of a wealthy couple and their dog, shows this skill. Van Eyck worked with thin layers of transparent color. Notice the light on the chandelier, the texture of the couple's clothes, and their reflection in the curved mirror behind them. The realistic detail is almost beyond belief. Paintings like this made Van Eyck famous across Europe. They made Naturalism more popular as well.

linear perspective: a technique for showing three-dimensional space on a flat surface. For instance, objects that are supposed to be closer to the viewer are larger than objects that are farther away.
oil paints: mixtures of pigment (color) with oil. The oil is often linseed oil, which comes from the dried seeds of the flax plant.

Parmigianino · *Self-Portrait in a Convex Mirror* · ca. 1523–1524
Kunsthistorisches Museum, Vienna, Austria

What is Mannerism?

The word Mannerism comes from an Italian word, *maniera*, which means "style." Earlier Renaissance artists had painted more realistically. But Mannerists were more interested in showing off their own style. They experimented with unnatural poses, proportions, and colors. They tried unusual settings and included mysterious details. In short, they weren't afraid to change or distort reality.

When and where was Mannerism popular?
The Mannerist style developed during the late Renaissance, lasting from about 1525 until 1600. Mannerism was centered in Italy. It flowered in the cities of Florence, Rome, and Venice.

Who are some of the most famous Mannerist painters?
Agnolo Bronzino, Italy, 1503–1572
Rosso Fiorentino, Italy, 1495–1540
El Greco, Greece, 1541–1614
Parmigianino, Italy, 1503–1540
Pontormo, Italy, 1494–1557
Jacopo Tintoretto, Italy, 1518–1594

What are some of Mannerism's most important characteristics?
–long, stretched-out figures
–odd or contorted poses and facial expressions
–imaginary settings
–unbalanced compositions
–unnatural colors or lighting

Why is this painting a good example of Mannerism?
Parmigianino painted *Self-Portrait in a Convex Mirror* when he was just twenty years old. It is an inventive example of Mannerism. The artist painted his reflection as it appeared in a convex (curved) mirror. To make the illusion more effective, he painted on a curved piece of wood. It's no accident that the most distorted part of this painting is Parmigianino's large hand—the same hand he used to create this stylized work.

compositions: how things are arranged on the canvas
contorted: twisted
distorted: exaggerated or made to look unnatural
proportions: how one part of something relates to another part or to the whole

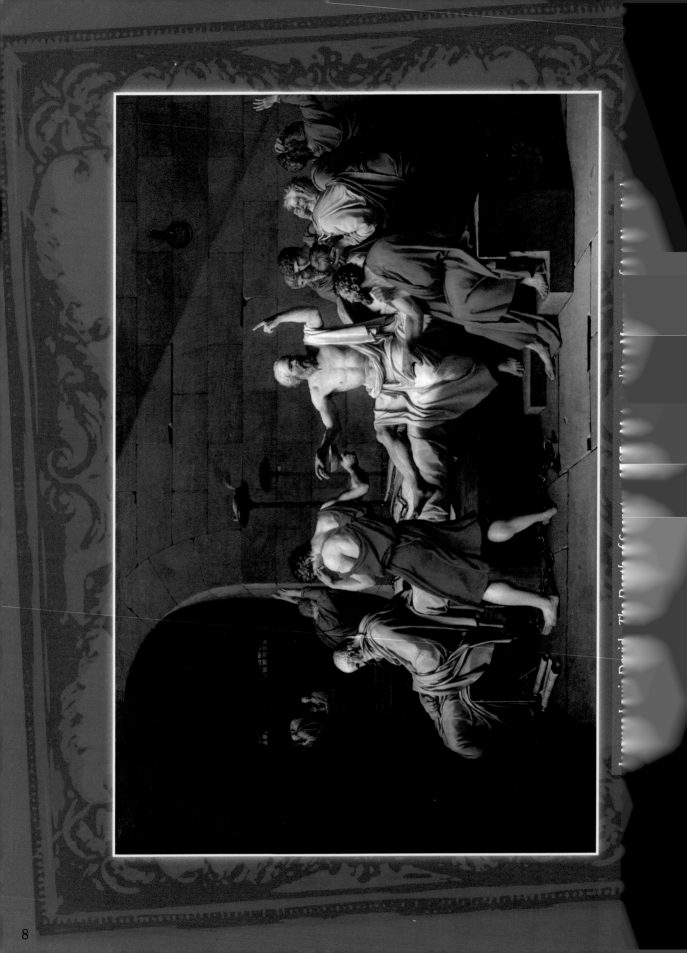

What is Neoclassicism?

Historians call ancient Greece and Rome "classical" civilizations. Classicism is a fancy way of saying that artists were inspired by ancient Greek and Roman art. A Classicism movement had already happened during the 1400s and 1500s. So the prefix "neo" was added, which meant this was a "new" classicism. Artists were especially inspired by discoveries of artifacts at the ancient Roman cities of Herculaneum and Pompeii. Both cities had been buried under volcanic ash during an eruption of Mount Vesuvius in A.D. 79.

When and where was Neoclassicism popular?
Neoclassicism was popular across Europe during the 1700s and early 1800s. This period was known as the Age of Reason. People believed in the power of science, nature, and logical thought. They challenged the power of kings and the Catholic Church. Artists modeled their work after the Greeks and Romans, whom they considered the first believers in the power of reason.

Who are some of the most famous Neoclassicist painters?
John Singleton Copley, United States, 1738–1815
Jacques-Louis David, France, 1748–1825
Jean-Auguste-Dominique Ingres, France, 1780–1867
Joshua Reynolds, Great Britain, 1723–1792
Benjamin West, United States, 1738–1820

What are some of Neoclassicism's most important characteristics?
–scenes from history or mythology (especially Greek or Roman)
–a hero at the center of the action
–a balanced and orderly composition
–a moral message

Why is this painting a good example of Neoclassicism?
In *The Death of Socrates*, Jacques-Louis David shows us a scene from Greek history. The Greek government had sentenced the philosopher Socrates to death for his teachings. His students planned an escape for him, but he refused. Socrates had agreed to live and die by society's rules. So he drank a cup of poison. This painting has both a hero and a moral message. Notice how the figures look as rigid as the ancient Roman statues unearthed at Pompeii.

mythology: stories told to express the beliefs of a group of people, to tell about gods and goddesses, or to give reasons for something in nature, such as what causes the sun to rise
philosopher: a person who studies wisdom, knowledge, truth, and the nature of reality

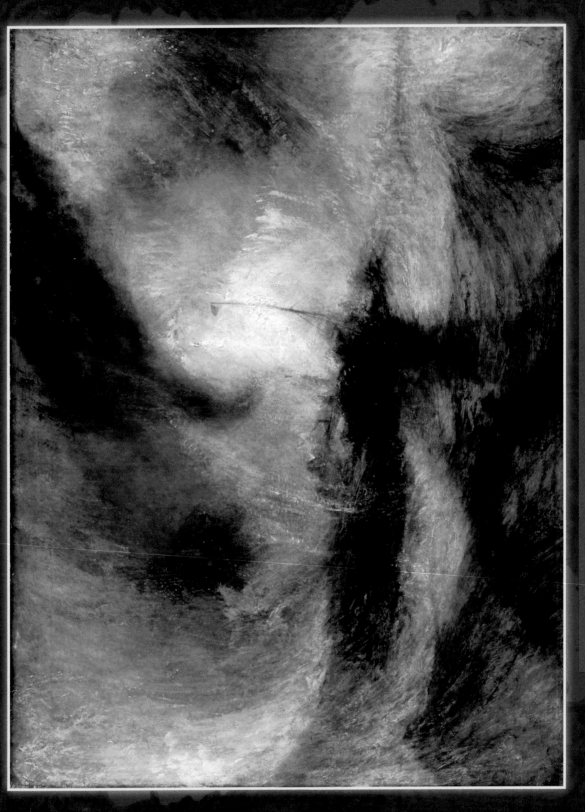

Joseph Mallord William Turner · *Snow Storm—Steam-Boat off a Harbour's Mouth* 1842 · Tate Gallery, London, England

What is Romanticism?

The people of Europe saw a lot of violence and bloodshed during the French Revolution (1789–1799) and the Napoleonic Wars (1799–1815). As a result, artists lost faith in the power of reason to improve the world. Romanticism was a reaction against Neoclassicism and reason. Romantic painters believed that feelings, instincts, and intuition were just as important as reason when creating art.

When and where was Romanticism popular?
Romanticism was widespread during the late 1700s and early 1800s, especially in western Europe. It was popular in Great Britain, France, Spain, Germany, and even extended to the United States.

Who are some of the most famous Romantic painters?
William Blake, Great Britain, 1757–1827

Eugène Delacroix, France, 1798–1863

Casper David Friedrich, Germany, 1774–1840

Théodore Géricault, France, 1791–1824

Francisco Goya, Spain, 1746–1828

Joseph Mallord William Turner, Great Britain, 1775–1851

What are some of Romanticism's most important characteristics?
–emphasized intuition, instinct, and imagination

–very emotional, moody, or spiritual

–fascinated with nature and landscapes

–often showed scenes of horror or the supernatural

Why is this painting a good example of Romanticism?
Joseph Turner once claimed he was tied to the mast of a boat in a snowstorm for four hours. After surviving the storm, he said, "I felt bound to record it." In his painting *Snow Storm—Steam-Boat off a Harbour's Mouth*, Turner imaginatively re-created the swirling snow and waves. He captured both the power of nature and the human emotions of fear and awe. Turner painted by instinct, breaking all the accepted rules. By doing so, he makes us feel the way he must have felt during the storm.

French Revolution: an uprising in France that ended rule by French King Louis XVI and started the formation of a new government

intuition: a feeling or idea that cannot be explained logically

Napoleonic Wars: a series of wars between France, led by Napoleon, and other countries in Europe

supernatural: something natural laws cannot explain, such as ghosts

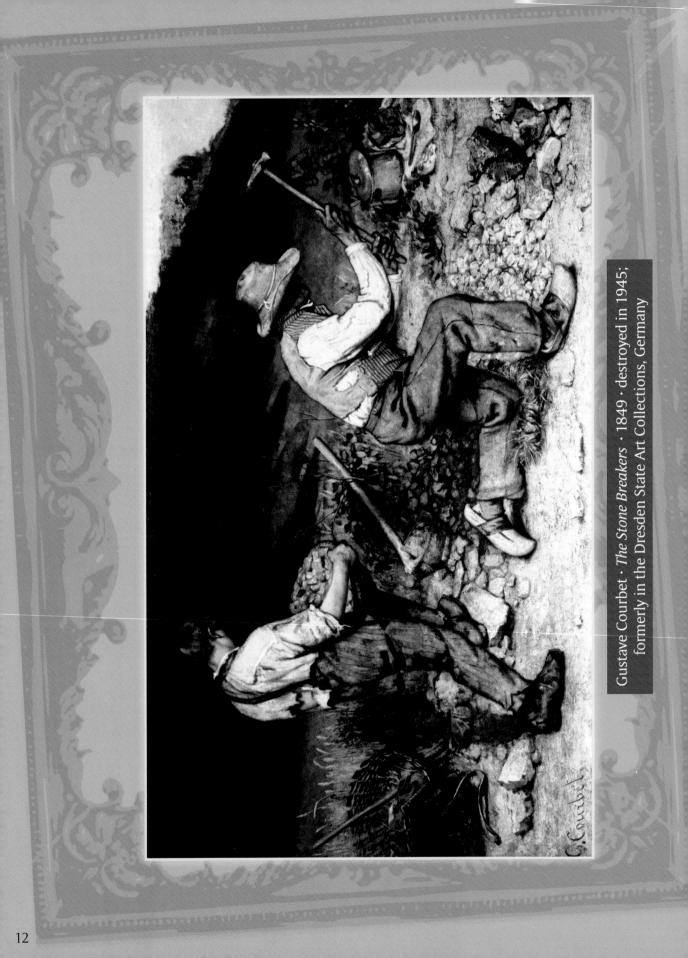

Gustave Courbet · *The Stone Breakers* · 1849 · destroyed in 1945; formerly in the Dresden State Art Collections, Germany

Until the mid-1800s, artists typically painted scenes from the Bible, heroes from classical mythology, or portraits of the rich. In doing so, they made life look better than it really was. The Realism movement focused on showing real life, with all of its dirtiness and ugliness. The Realists painted ordinary people doing everyday things.

When and where was Realism popular?
The Realism movement occurred mainly in France during the mid to late 1800s. A number of revolts had taken place across Europe in 1848. French artist Gustave Courbet felt the Romantic style was just an escape from realities such as poverty and war. He was the first to define Realism. The introduction of photography, which also showed the realities of everyday life, influenced this style.

Who are some of the most famous Realist painters?
Gustave Courbet, France, 1819–1877

Honoré Daumier, France, 1808–1879

Thomas Eakins, United States, 1844–1916

Jean-François Millet, France, 1814–1875

What are some of Realism's most important characteristics?
–ordinary people and everyday activities

–not idealized or romanticized

–sometimes ugly or distasteful subject matter

–implied criticism of social conditions

–influenced by photography

Why is this painting a good example of Realism?
In Courbet's painting, *The Stone Breakers*, he shows two dirty peasants working hard along a dusty road. The younger man, who struggles to lift a basket of rocks, wears a ripped shirt. The older man kneels, and his hat hides his face from the hot sun. This scene is not pretty, heroic, or inspirational—just ordinary, gritty, and real.

idealized: made to look ideal or perfect

Claude Monet · *Woman with a Parasol* · 1875 · National Gallery of Art, Washington, D.C.

What is Impressionism?

Like the Realists, the Impressionists preferred to paint scenes from everyday life. But they weren't interested in unpleasant things. They wanted to capture a moment, or a quick impression of a scene. The Impressionists often painted outdoors, where they could see the changing effects of light. And they painted spontaneously, using loose brushstrokes and mixing colors right on the canvas.

When and where was Impressionism popular?
Impressionism began in the 1860s in Paris, France. A group of artists who had been rejected by the official art authorities started sharing new ideas about art. They showed their work together, and gradually their ideas caught on. Impressionism was popular for about twenty years, until the mid-1880s.

Who are some of the most famous Impressionist painters?
Mary Cassatt, United States, 1844–1926

Claude Monet, France, 1840–1926

Berthe Morisot, France, 1841–1895

Camille Pissarro, France, 1830–1903

Pierre-Auguste Renoir, France, 1841–1919

Alfred Sisley, France, 1839–1899

What are some of Impressionism's most important characteristics?
–scenes from nature and everyday life

–painted outside

–quick, loose brushstrokes

–bright colors mixed right on the canvas

–spontaneous poses and unusual points of view

Why is this painting a good example of Impressionism?
Woman with a Parasol by Claude Monet is a painting of his wife, Camille, and their son, Jean. You don't have to look hard to see Monet's quick, loose brushstrokes, which he used masterfully to paint the summer wind. His colors are so bright you can almost feel the sunlight. Monet's point of view is from below, looking up—a view you might see through a camera. Sketchy and spontaneous, it captures his impression of this everyday scene.

spontaneous: happening all of a sudden; without previous thought or planning

Georges Seurat · *The Circus* · 1891 · Musée d'Orsay, Paris, France

What is Pointillism?

French painter Georges Seurat was interested in scientific theories on color, especially in how our eyes see color. He based Pointillism on those theories. In Pointillism, the artist applies paint in tiny dots, or points, of color. These points of color blend in the viewer's eyes to form new colors. For example, the painter might place a dot of red paint next to a dot of yellow paint. From a distance, these two colors blend to look like orange.

When and where was Pointillism popular?
Seurat and his friend Paul Signac developed Pointillism in France during the 1880s. Despite their enthusiasm, this style did not catch on with many other painters. They found the scientific ideas behind the style (and the technique of painting with tiny dots) too limiting.

Who are some of the most famous Pointillist painters?
Henri-Edmond Cross, France, 1856–1910
Camille Pissarro, France, 1830–1903
Georges Seurat, France, 1859–1891
Paul Signac, France, 1863–1935

What are some of Pointillism's most important characteristics?
–paint not mixed on a palette
–use of primary colors
–individual dots, or points, of color
–brushstrokes carefully placed, not spontaneous
–rigid compositions

Why is this painting a good example of Pointillism?
Although it is not finished, *The Circus* by Seurat is a wonderful example of Pointillism. If you look closely, you can see how he applied his paint in tiny dots and dashes of red, yellow, and blue. From a distance, our eyes blend these primary colors into the secondary colors orange, green, and purple. The result is a work of art that shimmers with light and color.

palette: a flat board on which an artist mixes paint
primary colors: red, yellow, and blue. These colors can be mixed to make all other colors.

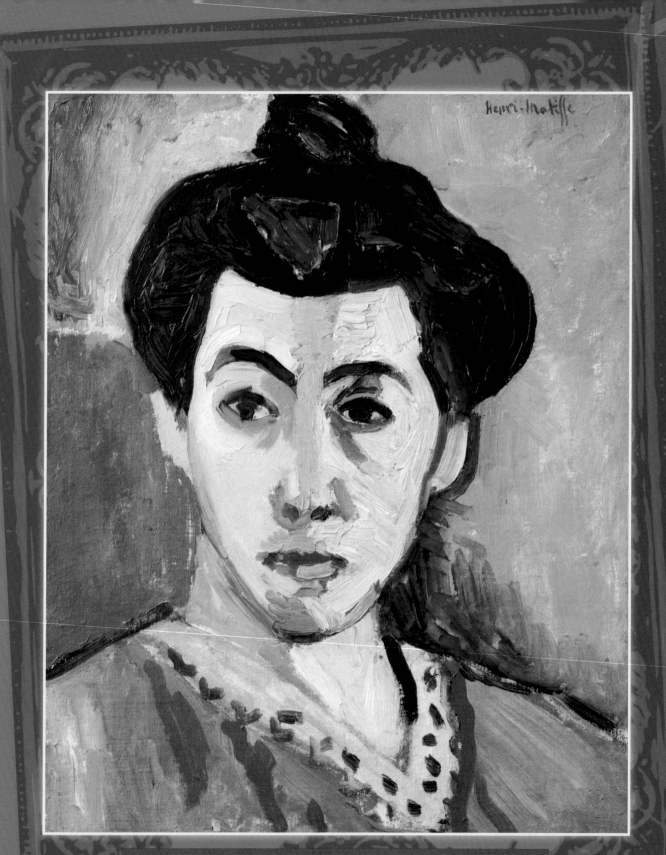

Henri Matisse · *Portrait of Madame Matisse (The Green Line)* · 1905
Statens Museum for Kunst, Copenhagen, Denmark

What is Fauvism?

The Fauvists wanted to show how they felt about what they were painting. Instead of using color realistically, they used color as a way to express their emotions. Because they also painted spontaneously, one critic called them "Les Fauves." This term means "the wild beasts" in French. Earlier artists—such as Vincent van Gogh and Paul Gauguin, who also painted with bold, emotional colors—influenced the Fauvists.

When and where was Fauvism popular?

All the Fauvists were French. Their bold style was born around 1898. It didn't really take off until the first Fauvist exhibition in Paris in 1905. By 1908 most Fauvists were moving on to other styles, such as Cubism.

Who are some of the most famous Fauvist painters?

André Derain, France, 1880–1954

Raoul Dufy, France, 1877–1953

Henri Matisse, France, 1869–1954

Georges Rouault, France, 1871–1958

Maurice de Vlaminck, France, 1876–1958

What are some of Fauvism's most important characteristics?

–bold, unnatural colors

–flat, unrealistic space

–quick, aggressive brushstrokes

–a rough, unfinished look

Why is this painting a good example of Fauvism?

Henri Matisse's *Portrait of Madame Matisse (The Green Line)* contains all the main elements of Fauvism. He painted half of the woman's face bright yellow and the other half reddish pink. He painted a green stripe down the middle. He also divided the background into three arbitrary areas of color: bright red, purple, and green. Looking at his brushstrokes, we can tell he painted quickly. Overall, Matisse's portrait is sketchy, flat, and unfinished looking. So why did Matisse paint this woman with such strange colors? Maybe they are the colors of love, since this is a portrait of his wife, Amelie.

arbitrary: seemingly random

Juan Gris · *Portrait of Pablo Picasso* · 1912 · The Art Institute of Chicago, Illinois

What is Cubism?

French painter Paul Cézanne planted the seeds of Cubism. He began by reducing everything he saw into basic shapes such as cylinders, spheres, and cubes. From there, Georges Braque and Pablo Picasso began taking things apart in their minds. Then they put the pieces back together on the canvas in an abstract form. Rather than showing one side of a thing, which is the way our eyes see, the Cubists wanted to show all sides of a thing at once.

When and where was Cubism popular?

Working as a team, French artist Georges Braque and Spanish artist Pablo Picasso developed Cubism between 1907 and 1914 in Paris. Their style revolutionized the art world. It became the most influential movement of the 1900s.

Who are some of the most famous Cubist painters?

Georges Braque, France, 1882–1963

Juan Gris, Spain, 1887–1927

Fernand Léger, France, 1881–1955

Pablo Picasso, Spain, 1881–1973

What are some of Cubism's most important characteristics?

–objects broken up and put back together in an abstract form

–all sides seen at once (multiple viewpoints)

–geometric shapes without realistic details

–fragmenting

–shallow space

–subdued colors

Why is this painting a good example of Cubism?

Juan Gris was Picasso's friend and neighbor. He was with Picasso and Braque as they developed Cubism. They inspired Gris to try the style for himself. *Portrait of Pablo Picasso* is one of his first attempts. The first thing you notice is how he broke up Picasso's face. The painting is full of abstract geometric shapes and fragments in quiet colors like blue and brown. But if you look closely, you can see that Picasso is holding a palette with small splotches of red, yellow, blue, and black.

abstract: unrecognizable subject matter in a work of art

subdued: dim, not bright

Umberto Boccioni · *The Street Enters the House* · 1911
Sprengel Museum, Hannover, Germany

WHAT IS FUTURISM?

Futurism celebrated the power and excitement of the machine age. The 1900s had just begun. Cities were becoming more industrial. The automobile and the airplane had recently been invented. In light of all this, the Futurists wanted to free themselves from the past and focus on everything that was new. Their subjects included trains, cars, cities, crowds, and people on the move.

When and where was Futurism popular?
Futurism was mainly an Italian art movement. It started in about 1909 and lasted until about 1918.

Who are some of the most famous Futurist painters?
Giacomo Balla, Italy, 1871–1958
Umberto Boccioni, Italy, 1882–1916
Carlo Carra, Italy, 1881–1966
Gino Severini, Italy, 1883–1966

What are some of Futurism's most important characteristics?
–power
–movement
–visual noise
–violence
–energy

The Futurists also borrowed techniques from Cubism, such as:
–breaking up and reassembling objects
–fragmenting
–multiple viewpoints

Why is this painting a good example of Futurism?
This painting by Umberto Boccioni is called *The Street Enters the House*. We can almost see the noise of modern life rushing toward the woman as she stands on her balcony. By using fragments, zigzagging angles, and bright colors, Boccioni shows the chaos and excitement of modern life.

visual noise: loud colors, harsh angles, and visual busyness

Max Ernst · *Forest and Dove* · 1927 · Tate Gallery, London, England

What is Surrealism?

The word *surrealism* comes from a French word meaning "super realism." The Surrealists wanted to create art that included their unconscious thoughts and dreams. Instead of thinking too much about what they were painting, they preferred to set their imaginations free. They experimented with different ways of being spontaneous.

When and where was Surrealism popular?

Surrealism developed in the mid-1920s and remained popular until the late 1930s. It began in Paris and spread across Europe and to the United States. Most art historians agree that after Cubism, Surrealism was the second most influential art movement of the 1900s.

Who are some of the most famous Surrealist painters?

Salvador Dali, Spain, 1904–1989

Max Ernst, Germany, 1891–1976

René Magritte, Belgium, 1898–1967

Joan Miró, Spain, 1893–1983

Yves Tanguy, France, 1900–1955

What are some of Surrealism's most important characteristics?

–the element of surprise

–free association

–uncensored thought

–dreamlike subject matter

–spontaneous techniques (automatic drawing, frottage, decalcomania)

Why is this painting a good example of Surrealism?

Max Ernst loved to use the element of chance. To create *Forest and Dove*, he covered his canvas with dark colors. Then he laid it paint-side down over a textured surface and scraped the back of the canvas with a palette knife. He called this technique *grattage*. The random pattern it made reminded Ernst of a forest, and the shape at the bottom looked like a cage. By adding a bird inside the cage, he gave the scene a strange, dreamlike quality.

automatic drawing: moving a pencil or brush randomly across the canvas
decalcomania: pressing textured material or objects into wet, painted canvas
frottage: a pencil rubbing made by putting paper over a textured surface
uncensored: not hidden
unconscious: something a person is not aware of

Jackson Pollock · *Enchanted Forest* · 1947
Guggenheim Museum, New York

What is Abstract Expressionism?

After World War II (1939–1945), American artists wanted to remind the world of our common humanity. Abstract Expressionism was their attempt to express emotions that anyone could relate to. Abstract Expressionism includes many different styles, but they all seem to express the way people feel about the fast pace and confusion of modern society.

When and where was Abstract Expressionism popular?

Abstract Expressionism was born in New York City during the late 1940s. It remained popular until the late 1950s. It helped New York replace Paris as the new center of the art world. Art historians say Abstract Expressionism is the most original style ever created in the United States. It continues to influence artists to this day.

Who are some of the most famous Abstract Expressionist painters?

Willem de Kooning, Netherlands, 1904–1997

Barnett Newman, United States, 1905–1970

Robert Motherwell, United States, 1915–1991

Jackson Pollock, United States, 1912–1956

Mark Rothko, Russia, 1903–1970

Clyfford Still, United States, 1904–1980

What are some of Abstract Expressionism's most important characteristics?

–large canvases

–all areas of the painting are equally important

–abstract

–emphasizes the physical process of painting

–loaded with emotion

–spontaneous

Why is this painting a good example of Abstract Expressionism?

Jackson Pollock's *Enchanted Forest* is large—more than 7 feet (2.1 meters) tall and almost 4 feet (1.2 m) wide. He created it by laying his canvas on the floor, then pouring and dripping paint on it while walking and dancing around it. This technique is called action painting. Because it's abstract, *Enchanted Forest* doesn't really look like a forest. But the swirling lines of paint do remind us of tangled tree branches and vines.

Expressionism: any art that expresses intense emotion, usually by distorting reality. An Expressionism movement took place from about 1905 to 1925.

Victor Vasarely · *Composition with Red Squares* · ca. 1969–1970
Musée Vasarely, Gordes, France

What is Op Art?

The word *op* is short for "optical." It comes from the fact that this style is based on optical illusions. Most Op Art paintings are made up of abstract geometric patterns. They exist mainly to fool your eye. The idea behind Op Art is to explore how our eyes see. Some Op Art paintings are so vibrant and dynamic, they make your eyes hurt!

When and where was Op Art popular?
Op Art probably started with a work called *Zebra*, which Hungarian artist Victor Vasarely created in 1938. However, Op Art became most popular during the late 1960s in the United States and Europe after an exhibition of Op Art paintings appeared at New York City's Museum of Modern Art in 1965.

Who are some of the most famous Op Art painters?
Richard Anuszkiewicz, United States, 1930–
M. C. Escher, Netherlands, 1898–1972
Bridget Riley, Great Britain, 1931–
Victor Vasarely, Hungary, 1908–1997

What are some of Op Art's most important characteristics?
–movement
–vibration
–warping
–bulging
–flashing

These effects are achieved through the use of:
–repeated geometric shapes and patterns
–perspective (some parts look closer than others)
–contrasting colors (or black and white)

Why is this painting a good example of Op Art?
At first glance, Victor Vasarely's *Composition with Red Squares* simply looks like boxy shapes that are intertwined. But the longer you look, the more things change. One minute, corners seem to be coming towards us. The next minute, the very same corners seem to be moving away from us. Vasarely achieved this "back and forth" effect by cleverly using pattern, perspective, contrasting colors, and shading. As you can see, this is art that gives your eyes a workout.

bulging: the appearance that something is coming closer to the viewer
flashing: a flickering effect caused by repeated patterns and contrasting colors
warping: the appearance that a shape is twisted or distorted

Audrey Flack · *Marilyn* · 1977 · The University of Arizona Museum of Art, Tucson

What is Photorealism?

Photorealism is the art of painting from a photograph, instead of from life. The Photorealists liked how a photo captures a single moment in time. They were skilled at simulating the reflections, complex geometry, and tiny details shown in photographs. It's often hard to tell whether their finished works are paintings or photos.

When and where was Photorealism popular?
Photorealism was most popular in the United States during the late 1960s and 1970s. The Photorealists were reacting against the abstract direction that art had taken. They wanted to get back to painting recognizable subject matter.

Who are some of the most famous Photorealist painters?
Robert Bechtle, United States, 1932–
Charles Bell, United States, 1935–1995
Don Eddy, United States, 1944–
Richard Estes, United States, 1936–
Audrey Flack, United States, 1931–
Ralph Goings, United States, 1928–

What are some of Photorealism's most important characteristics?
–worked from photographs
–used slide projectors or grids to transfer images onto canvas
–made direct copies of photographs, but usually larger
–focused on cityscapes, portraits, and still lifes
–often used an airbrush to hide brush marks

Why is this painting a good example of Photorealism?
Marilyn is one of Audrey Flack's most famous works. First, she assembled a still life using various objects that had symbolic meaning for her. These include makeup, fresh fruit, and a photo of Marilyn Monroe. Then Flack took a photographic slide of the still life and projected it onto her canvas. Finally, she painted directly over the projected slide image. This slide projection technique, combined with her use of an airbrush, is what gives her work such an amazingly Photorealistic look.

airbrush: a tool used to apply paint in a fine spray
still lifes: paintings of objects that don't move, such as fruit or flowers

Photo Acknowledgements

Cover art courtesy of: © akg-images/Sprengel Museum (top left); © National Gallery Collection; By kind permission of the Trustees of the National Gallery, London/CORBIS (top right); © iStockphoto.com/Marie-france Bélanger (center); © Erich Lessing/Art Resource, NY (bottom left); © Réunion des Musées Nationaux/Art Resource, NY (bottom right).

Interior art courtesy of: Page 1 and all backgrounds: © iStockphoto.com/Marie-france Bélanger; Page 4: © National Gallery Collection; By kind permission of the Trustees of the National Gallery, London/CORBIS; Page 6: © Erich Lessing/Art Resource, NY; Page 8: David, Jacques Louis (1748–1825), *The Death of Socrates*, 1787, oil on canvas, 51 x 77¼ in. (129.5 x 196.2 cm), Catherine Lorillard Wolfe Fund, 1931 (31.45), The Metropolitan Museum of Art, New York, NY. Image copyright © The Metropolitan Museum of Art/Art Resource, NY; Page 10: © Clore Collection, Tate Gallery, London/Art Resource, NY; Page 12: *The Stone Breakers*, 1849 (oil on canvas) (destroyed in 1945), Courbet, Gustave (1819–77)/ Galerie Neue Meister, Dresden, Germany, © Staatliche Kunstsammlungen Dresden/The Bridgeman Art Library International; Page 14: Claude Monet, *Woman with a Parasol - Madame Monet and Her Son*, Collection of Mr. and Mrs. Paul Mellon, Image © Board of Trustees, National Gallery of Art, Washington DC; Page 16: © Réunion des Musées Nationaux/Art Resource, NY; Page 18: © 2008 Succession H. Matisse, Paris/Artists Rights Society (ARS), New York. Henri Matisse, *Portrait of Madame Matisse (The Green Line)*, 1905. 40.5 x 32.5 cm. Oil and tempera on canvas. Statens Museum for Kunst, Photograph © SMK Foto; Page 20: Juan Gris, Spanish, 1887-1927, *Portrait of Pablo Picasso*, 1912, oil on canvas, 36¾ x 29¼ in. (93.3 x 74.3 cm), Gift of Leigh B. Block, 1958.525, The Art Institute of Chicago. Photography © The Art Institute of Chicago; Page 22: © akg-images/Sprengel Museum; Page 24: © 2008 Artists Rights Society (ARS), New York/ADAGP, Paris. Image © Tate Gallery, London/Art Resource, NY; Page 26: © 2008 The Pollock-Krasner Foundation/Artists Rights Society (ARS), New York. Image © Alinari/Art Resource, NY; Page 28: © 2008 Artists Rights Society (ARS), New York/ADAGP, Paris. Image © Erich Lessing/Art Resource, NY; Page 30: AUDREY FLACK, *"Marilyn (Vanitas)"*, 1977, oil over acrylic on canvas, 96 x 96 inches, Courtesy Louis K. Meisel Gallery, New York. Collection of The University of Arizona Museum of Art, Tucson, Museum Purchase with funds provided by the Edward J. Gallagher, Jr. Memorial Fund.